*Poetry by Ted Hughes*

*The Hawk in the Rain (1957)*
*Lupercal (1960)*
*Wodwo (1967)*
*Crow (1971)*
*Seneca's Oedipus (1972)*
*Gaudete (1977)*
*Cave Birds (1978)*
*Remains of Elmet (1979)*
*Moortown (1980)*
*New Selected Poems (1982)*
*River (1984)*
*Flowers and Insects (1986)*
*Wolfwatching (1991)*

# Wolfwatching

# Ted Hughes

# Wolfwatching

*The Noonday Press*

*Farrar, Straus and Giroux*

*New York*

14194

*For Hilda*

# Contents

# Wolfwatching

## A Sparrow Hawk

Slips from your eye-corner—overtaking
Your first thought.

Through your mulling gaze over haphazard earth
The sun's cooled carbon wing
Whets the eye-beam.

Those eyes in their helmet
Still wired direct
To the nuclear core—they alone

Laser the lark-shaped hole
In the lark's song.

You find the fallen spurs, among soft ashes.

And maybe you find him

Materialized by twilight and dew
Still as a listener—

The warrior

Blue shoulder-cloak wrapped about him,
Leaning, hunched,
Among the oaks of the harp.

# Two Astrological Conundrums

## I. The Fool's Evil Dream

I was walking about.
Trees here, trees there, ferny accompaniment.
Rocks sticking through their moss jerseys.
A twilight like smoked spectacles, depressive.

I saw a glowing beast—a tigress.
Only different with flower smells, wet-root smells,
Fish-still-alive-from-their-weed-river smells
And eyes that hurt me with beauty.

She wanted to play so we gambolled.
She promised to show me her cave
Which was the escape route from death
And which came out into a timeless land.

To find this cave, she said, we lie down
And you hold me, so, and we fly.
So it was I came to be folded
In the fur of a tiger. And as we travelled

She told me of a very holy man
Who fed himself to a tigress
Because hunger had dried up her milk
And as he filled her belly he became

The never-dying god who gives everything
Which he had always wanted to be.
As I heard her story I dissolved
In the internal powers of tiger

And passed through a dim land
Swinging under her backbone. Till I heard
A sudden cry of terror, an infant's cry—
Close, as if my own ear had cried it.

I sat up
Wet and alone
Among starry rocks.

A bright spirit went away weeping.

## II. Tell

This was my dream. Suddenly my old steel bow
Sprang into my hand and my whole body
Leaned into the bend a harp frame
Strung so perfectly it seemed weightless.

I saw the Raven sitting alone
On the crest of the globe. I could see
The Raven's eye agleam in the sky river
Like an emblem on a flowing banner.

I saw the Raven's eye watching me
Through the slitted fabric of the skyflow.
I bent the bow's full weight against the star
In that eye until I could see nothing

But that star. Then as I sank my aim
Deeper into the star that had grown
To fill the Universe I heard a whisper:
'Be careful. I'm here. Don't forget me.'

With all my might—I hesitated.

## Slump Sundays

Humped around me, mourners ate cold mutton,
Or maybe tripe, ham, piccalilli,
Sliced onions in vinegar, pickled beetroots,
Bread, jam, cheese, cakes, tea—

Something stirred in the half-light.
The tea stirred it. The valley god
Was pulling itself together
In the smokers' haze. Then a mushroomy whiff

Soured off the wet mills.
Souls were mouldering
Inside those great barns—the seed-corn
Lugged back from the Somme.

It served for a mother-tongue. Oracular spore-breath
Of a kind of fungus:
The homegrown hallucinogen
Of a visionary defeat.

Inhaling it, I came to
Under a rainy ridge, in a goblin clump
Of agaric.
Girlish birches waved at the window.

And a scraggy sheep at the moor-edge
Like a boulder tipped from the quarry
Took on the wild look of a hope
Returning from no man's land.

## Climbing into Heptonstall

The Tourist Guide, with his Group, in the ring of horizons,
Looked down on to Hebden. 'You will notice
How the walls are black.'
                              'Wash the black walls!'
Came the madman's yell. Bird-like. Wordless.

It meant: 'Wash the blood
Wash the Calder
Of all that still weeps down
Out of the walls

The weaver's baffled, half-deaf shout
Congealed in the walls

The birth–death confinement
A candle over the psalms
The breathed-in and breathed-out
Sour odour of mould
In the survival cells

Soots of the cold
And substitute
Flame lit by Wesley.

So spring-clean the skull. Sweep from the soul's attic
Spinners, weavers, tacklers, dyers, and their infants.
All agitators of wool and cotton
Caught in the warp and the woof. In a nook of the hills,

In the web of the streets (the Mill's own web)—
All the jackets that hung there, the prayers that twitched!
And in the web of the Chapel (the graveyard web)—
The shiver of empty names! So scrub

The stomach lining, rid it
Of the arthritic and vinegar cud
Of their swallowed heart-burn. "Penny-hunger",
That anaesthetic herb, choked this valley.
Spirit-flower of a stone-deep deprivation.
Rampant—perennial—their one plenty. So
Burn the record break the monument.
Time broke their machine. Let forgetting
Ease down the old gut of the glacier.
Let the seas recycle their atoms.

What survived
Nothing's left
Barely a temper
Less than a nothing
                    a hymn, a hymn
Of going
Without
Without
Without—'
                    And he kicked up his legs,
A clowning dance, and let out a tuneless yodel:

'This is what made the wild harebell
So beautifully witless.
The trout under the stone so light-hearted!'

Then his voice hardened—to a wail

And he lurched off, bird-faced, stiff-kneed, downhill.
    The Guide
Half-smiled, recovering his flock. And,
With an opening sweep of his arm:
                              'Before us—
Stands yesterday.'

*The Punishment of Iago, Re-incarnated*
*as Malvolio in the Form of*
**A Macaw**


Sorcerer! How you hate it all!
Trampling it under slowly—kneading it all
To an ectoplasmic pulp.

Your trampling is your dance. With your eye—
Your head-writhing
Evil eye—fixing the enemy,

You writhe you weave you entangle
All the cords of his soul
And so drag him towards you, and trample him under.

Gomorrah! Sodom! Your eye squirms on its pin
In its socket of ashes. In the sulphurous hand-axe
You have to use for a face. That cowl,

That visor of black flint,
Is also your third foot. And your flint cup
Serves you for under-jaw, crudely chipped to fit.

Such a pale eye will never forgive!
The egg-daub daffodil shirt
Is no consolation. And that puppet

Prussian-blue hauberk of feathers
Is a mockery.

                    Nothing will help, you know,
When you come, finally, to grips

With the dancing stars
Who devised this
Trembling degradation and prison and this

Torture instrument of brittle plastic
Jammed askew
Athwart your gullet.

# Dust As We Are

My post-war father was so silent
He seemed to be listening. I eavesdropped
On the hot line. His lonely sittings
Mangled me, in secret—like TV
Watched too long, my nerves lasered.
Then, an after-image of the incessant
Mowing passage of machine-gun effects,
What it filled a trench with. And his laugh
(How had that survived—so nearly intact?)
Twitched the curtain never quite deftly enough
Over the hospital wards
Crowded with his (photographed) shock-eyed pals.

I had to use up a lot of spirit
Getting over it. I was helping him.
I was his supplementary convalescent.
He took up his pre-war *joie de vivre*.
But his displays of muscular definition
Were a bleached montage—lit landscapes:
Swampquakes of the slime of puddled soldiers
Where bones and bits of equipment
Showered from every shell-burst.
                                        Naked men
Slithered staring where their mothers and sisters
Would never have to meet their eyes, or see
Exactly how they sprawled and were trodden.

So he had been salvaged and washed.
His muscles very white—marble white.

He had been heavily killed. But we had revived him.
Now he taught us a silence like prayer.
There he sat, killed but alive—so long
As we were very careful. I divined,
With a comb,
Under his wavy, golden hair, as I combed it,
The fragility of skull. And I filled
With his knowledge.
                              After mother's milk
This was the soul's food. A soap-smell spectre
Of the massacre of innocents. So the soul grew.
A strange thing, with rickets—a hyena.
No singing—that kind of laughter.

# Wolfwatching

Woolly-bear white, the old wolf
Is listening to London. His eyes, withered in
Under the white wool, black peepers,
While he makes nudging, sniffing offers
At the horizon of noise, the blue-cold April
Invitation of airs. The lump of meat
Is his confinement. He has probably had all his life
Behind wires, fraying his eye-efforts
On the criss-cross embargo. He yawns
Peevishly like an old man and the yawn goes
Right back into Kensington and there stops
Floored with glaze. Eyes
Have worn him away. Children's gazings
Have tattered him to a lumpish
Comfort of woolly play-wolf. He's weary.
He curls on the cooling stone
That gets heavier. Then again the burden
Of a new curiosity, a new testing
Of new noises, new people with new colours
Are coming in at the gate. He lifts
The useless weight and lets it sink back,
Stirring and settling in a ball of unease.
All his power is a tangle of old ends,
A jumble of leftover scraps and bits of energy
And bitten-off impulses and dismantled intuitions.
He can't settle. He's ruffling
And re-organizing his position all day
Like a sleepless half-sleep of growing agonies
In a freezing car. The day won't pass.

The night will be worse. He's waiting
For the anaesthetic to work
That has already taken his strength, his beauty
And his life.

He levers his stiffness erect
And angles a few tottering steps
Into his habits. He goes down to water
And drinks. Age is thirsty. Water
Just might help and ease. What else
Is there to do? He tries to find again
That warm position he had. He cowers
His hind legs to curl under him. Subsides
In a trembling of wolf-pelt he no longer
Knows how to live up to.
                              And here
Is a young wolf, still intact.
He knows how to lie, with his head,
The Asiatic eyes, the gunsights
Aligned effortless in the beam of his power.
He closes his pale eyes and is easy,
Bored easy. His big limbs
Are full of easy time. He's waiting
For the chance to live, then he'll be off.
Meanwhile the fence, and the shadow-flutter
Of moving people, and the roller-coaster
Roar of London surrounding, are temporary,
And cost him nothing, and he can afford

To prick his ears to all that and find nothing
As to forest. He still has the starlings
To amuse him. The scorched ancestries,
Grizzled into his back, are his royalty.
The rufous ears and neck are always ready.
He flops his heavy running paws, resplays them
On pebbles, and rests the huge engine
Of his purring head. A wolf
Dropped perfect on pebbles. For eyes
To put on a pedestal. A product
Without a market.

                      But all the time
The awful thing is happening: the iron inheritance,
The incredibly rich will, torn up
In neurotic boredom and eaten,
Now indigestible. All that restlessness
And lifting of ears, and aiming, and re-aiming
Of nose, is like a trembling
Of nervous breakdown, afflicted by voices.
Is he hearing the deer? Is he listening
To gossip of non-existent forest? Pestered
By the hour-glass panic of lemmings
Dwindling out of reach? He's run a long way
Now to find nothing and be patient.
Patience is suffocating in all those folds
Of deep fur. The fairy tales
Grow stale all around him
And go back into pebbles. His eyes

Keep telling him all this is real
And that he's a wolf—of all things
To be in the middle of London, of all
Futile, hopeless things. Do Arctics
Whisper on their wave-lengths—fantasy-draughts
Of escape and freedom? His feet,
The power-tools, lie in front of him—
He doesn't know how to use them. Sudden
Dramatic lift and re-alignment
Of his purposeful body—
                    the Keeper
Has come to freshen the water.

And the prodigious journeys
Are thrown down again in his
Loose heaps of rope.
The future's snapped and coiled back
Into a tangled lump, a whacking blow
That's damaged his brain. Quiet,
Amiable in his dogginess,
Disillusioned—all that preparation
Souring in his skin. His every yawn
Is another dose of poison. His every frolic
Releases a whole flood
Of new hopelessness which he then
Has to burn up in sleep. A million miles
Knotted in his paws. Ten million years
Broken between his teeth. A world
Stinking on the bone, pecked by sparrows.

He's hanging
Upside down on the wire
Of non-participation.
He's a tarot-card, and he knows it.
He can howl all night
And dawn will pick up the same card
And see him painted on it, with eyes
Like doorframes in a desert
Between nothing and nothing.

## Telegraph Wires

Take telegraph wires, a lonely moor,
And fit them together. The thing comes alive in your ear.

Towns whisper to towns over the heather.
But the wires cannot hide from the weather.

So oddly, so daintily made
It is picked up and played.

Such unearthly airs
The ear hears, and withers!

In the revolving ballroom of space,
Bowed over the moor, a bright face

Draws out of telegraph wires the tones
That empty human bones.

# Source

Where did all those tears come from?
Were they the natural spring?
He'd returned, happiness,
He'd won the war. End of the table
Every evening, so bursting with presence
He alarmed his children. What were your tears
Looking for? Something you'd lost? Something
Still hurting? Or
You'd got into a habit,
Maybe during the war, of connecting yourself
To something beyond life, a mourning
That repaired you
And was necessary. You were so happy
Your sisters-in-law lived embittered
With envy of you. Hadn't your tears heard?
The sparrows on the chimney
Cared nothing for God,
Did without the grief-bump,
Tear-ducts, they simply went plop
When your eldest shot them, and dropped backwards
Into the soot-hole. Your sorrowing
Was its own blindness. Or was it
Blinded with tears of the future? Your future,
Fulfilling your most secret prayers, laid wrinkles
Over your face as honours. Your tears didn't care.
They'd come looking for you
Wherever you sat alone. They would find you
(Just as I did
On those thundery, stilled afternoons

Before my schooldays). You would be bowed
In your workroom, over your sewing machine.
They would snuggle against you. You would
Stop the needle and without a word
Begin to weep quietly. Like a singing.
With no other care, only to weep
Wholly, deeply, as if at last
You had arrived, as if now at last
You could rest, could relax utterly
Into a luxury of pure weeping—
Could dissolve yourself, me, everything
Into this relief of your strange music.

# Sacrifice

Born at the bottom of the heap. And as he grew upwards
The welts of his brow deepened, fold upon fold.
Like the Tragic Mask.
Cary Grant was his living double.

They said: When he was little he'd drop
And kick and writhe, and kick and cry:
'I'll break my leg! I'll break my leg!'
Till he'd ground his occiput bald.

While the brothers built cords, moleskins, khakis
Into dynastic, sweated ziggurats,
His fateful forehead sank
Away among Westerns, the ruts of the Oregon Trail.

Screwdriver, drill, chisel, saw, hammer
Were less than no use.
A glass-fronted cabinet was his showpiece.
His wife had locked him in there with the china.

His laugh jars at my ear. That laugh
Was an elastic vault into freedom.
Sound as a golfball.
He'd belt it into the blue.

He never drank in a bar. When he stood
Before he'd stepped she'd plumped the cushions
        beneath him.

So perfectly kept.
Sundays they drove here and there in the car.

An armchair Samson. Baffled and shorn,
His dream bulged into forearms
That performed their puppet-play of muscles
To make a nephew stare. He and I

Lammed our holly billets across Banksfields—
A five-inch propeller climbing the skylines
For two, three seconds—to the drop. And the paced-out
    length
Of his leash! The limit of human strength!

Suddenly he up and challenged
His brothers for a third of the partnership.
The duumvirate of wives turned down their thumbs.
Brotherly concern—Rain from Rochdale!

Snow from Halifax! Stars over valley walls!
His fireside escape
Simple as leaping astride a bare-back pinto
Was a kick at the ceiling, and that laugh.

He toiled in his attic after midnight
Mass-producing toy ducks
On wooden wheels, that went with clicks.
Flight! Flight!

The brothers closed their eyes. They quivered their jowls:
British Columbia's the place for a chap like thee!
The lands of the future! Look at Australia—
Crying out for timber buildings! Get out there!

On the canal bridge bend, at Hawkscluffe,
A barrel bounced off a lorry,
His motorbike hit the wall.
'I just flew straight up—and when I dropped

I missed the canal! I actually missed the canal!
I nearly broke the bank! For once
I landed smack on my feet!
My shoelaces burst from top to bottom!'

His laugh thumped my body.
When he tripped
The chair from beneath him, in his attic,
Midsummer dusk, his sister, forty miles off,

Cried out at the hammer blow on her nape.
And his daughter
Who'd climbed up to singsong: 'Supper, Daddy'
Fell back down the stairs to the bottom.

## For the Duration

I felt a strange fear when the war-talk,
Like a creeping barrage, approached you.
Jig and jag I'd fitted much of it together.
Our treasure, your D.C.M.—again and again
Carrying in the wounded
Collapsing with exhaustion. And as you collapsed
A shell-burst
Just in front of you lifting you upright
For the last somnambulist yards
Before you fell under your load into the trench.
The shell, some other time, that buried itself
Between your feet as you walked
And thoughtfully failed to go off.
The shrapnel hole, over your heart—how it spun you.
The blue scar of the bullet at your ankle
From a traversing machine-gun that tripped you
As you cleared the parapet. Meanwhile
The horrors were doled out, everybody
Had his appalling tale.
But what alarmed me most
Was your silence. Your refusal to tell.
I had to hear from others
What you survived and what you did.

Maybe you didn't want to frighten me.
Now it's too late.
Now I'd ask you shamelessly.
But then I felt ashamed.
What was my shame? Why couldn't I have borne

To hear you telling what you underwent?
Why was your war so much more unbearable
Than anybody else's? As if nobody else
Knew how to remember. After some uncle's
Virtuoso tale of survival
That made me marvel and laugh—
I looked at your face, your cigarette
Like a dial-finger. And my mind
Stopped with numbness.

Your day-silence was the coma
Out of which your night-dreams rose shouting.
I could hear you from my bedroom—
The whole hopelessness still going on,
No man's land still crying and burning
Inside our house, and you climbing again
Out of the trench, and wading back into the glare

As if you might still not manage to reach us
And carry us to safety.

# Anthem for Doomed Youth

*He gave us the morning star,*
*The medicine bag*
*Swagged with forests and rivers, and the game*
*Quaking the earth like a drum.*


8th, 9th, 10th, 11th of August,
The rifle elated,
The Ford in third, the climb out
Over the top towards Oxenhope.

And again, over the top towards Burnley,
Days heather plumped to the macadam.
All adolescence there, still tucked intact
Into the magazine of the rifle.

Who owned the moors? O we did!
The Mighty Gitchimanitou, in our tent,
Had handed us the charter—
Blowing Lord Savile's feather off it.

Heads cocked for the Law
We crawled
Through the war's drizzling afterdawn
In the utility makeshift early fifties.

You there, manly from Africa,
Steadying the dodgy globe of your future
As you lined up, quiet-eyed,
Backsight and foresight.

But who's that in the back seat?
Blondy curls, blue lamps—
Your soul, a warm egg,
In her beringed fist.

And who's that other beside her?
And what does she hold
In her broody fingers?
It was a bumper year for the portly birds.

Our switching glances, shadow-low,
Hawked across the purple,
And the tame, fuddled coveys
Trickled up their ginnels, to outlooks—

Lighthouses swivelling their simple minds,
Surprised by darkness,
Dropped to numbers,
Fluffing together in the boot.

Crack! And the echo: Crack! Dumb and deaf
The Winchester 69's
Dialogue with history. It woke us.
Conscripts of a dream! The dream broke there.

Only the dodo birds
Trooped up
And fell open—
Suddenly big, dark-hearted poppies.

# The Black Rhino

*I.*

This is the Black Rhino, the elastic boulder, coming at a
    gallop.
The boulder with a molten core, the animal missile,
Enlarging towards you. This is him in his fame—

Whose past is Behemoth, sixty million years printing the
    strata
Whose present is the brain-blink behind a recoiling
    gunsight
Whose future is a cheap watch shaken in your ear

Listen—bedrock accompanies him, a drumbeat
But his shadow over the crisp tangle of grass-tips
    hesitates, passes, hesitates, passes lightly
As a moth at noon

For this is the Black Rhino, who vanishes as he approaches
Every second there is less and less of him
By the time he reaches you nothing will remain, maybe, but
    the horn—an ornament for a lady's lap

Quick, now, the light is perfect for colour—catch the wet,
    mud caul, compact of extinct forms, that protects his
    blood from the rays
Video the busy thirst of his hair-fringed ears drinking
    safety from the burnt air
Get a shot of his cocked tail carrying its own little torch
    of courageous whiskers

Zoom in on the lava peephole where prehistory peers from
    the roots of his horn
(Every moment more and more interested)
Get a close-up of his horn

Which is an electric shock to your bootsoles (you bowed
    over your camera), as if a buried thing burst from
    beneath you, as if he resurrected beneath you,
Erupting from dust and thorns,
At a horn-down gallop, the hieroglyph of amazement—

Quickly, quick, or even as you stare
He will have dissolved
Into a gagging stench, in the shimmer.

Bones will come out on the negative.

## II.

This vision came
To a man asleep
Over a book
Beside his candle.
A beast came up
Into the flame
As into the dock.
The sleeper spoke:

'I have to laugh.
You stand accused
And convicted
Of being born
The Unicorn,
God's other Child
Whose nature heals
With earthlier stuff,
But just the same
To be sacrificed—
That opiate beast
Worshipped by
The humbly addicted
Bodily ills
And misery
Of the whole East:
Your every grain
Both anodyne
And Eucharist.

No wonder man
Craving his drug
Divides you small,
Strips every scrap
And bloody rag
Off your wraith,
Hooked on his faith
Or senile hope
Your relics will heal
And restore all.

And carves your horn
To adorn
The dagger that stands
His touchy pride's
Totem pole—
The sentinel
Over the hole
Of his navel
And what it hides.

You are to blame.
With your horn's length
You have nailed your strength
To Eden's coffin
Tree, the tree
Of sophistry,
Too solidly

To tug yourself free.
So now you die.'

Already dead
The Rhino cried
From a puddle of blood
Almost dried
In the African dust:
'What can you know
Of wrong or right,
Of evil or good?
You are the crime.
I accept
I no more exist
Outside your dream
And lethal whim
Of what I am
Than the Beetle can—
Though on many a plaque
Where the dead go
Beneath Egypt
The rising sun
And horn of light—
Be other than black.'

Then the man sighed
And sniffed the waft
Of a candle snuffed

And lay back in the crypt
Of his time-warped skull
Under a wall
Where long ago
The Rhino had left
Its lowly name
As a silhouette
Writ in soot.

*III.*

The Black Rhino is vanishing.
Horribly sick, without knowing,

She is vanishing. She is infected
With the delusions of man. She has become a delusion.

Every cell of her body is ruptured with human delusion.
She is vanishing

Into a hallucination. She has blundered somehow into
      man's phantasmagoria, and cannot get out.
Even the Ox-pecker cries in fear and the White Egret
      snatches away his shadow.

The Black Rhino wheels and is baffled. Who can help her?
Feints of delirium flush under her crusty wraps of sunned
      clay where the flies dig for a way in

The first fatal tokens prickle awake
A torn wisp of stars—a free-fall glimpse of the constellated
      night-bazaars of Japan and Indo-China—blinding migraine

Waves of nausea ripples of mirage
A sensation about the mouth of oiled euphoria, while fifty
      thousand North Yemenite warrior youths come of age
      in the camera (the same number as next year)

The symptoms far-fetched but exact
Each gripping a dagger by the hilt of rhino horn at eight
      or nine thousand dollars a handful

The Black Rhino snatched at by terrors
Stares into the black hole in her head, is it hunger in the
    electron anti-matter basic void

A bat's eye view of Dubai, counting the dhows in the bay,
    flitting from bedroom to bedroom, counting the notes
    in the wallets and the purses
And taking a turn between the sheets

Feels the undertow of abyss a spinning
Is vanishing

Sways blurs in her outline tries to hear
Tries to hold on to the cool wallow of her earthenware self,
    the mouthful of thorns, the superb, mauling brawls of
    courtship, the monumental couplings

Hypnagogic shouts jabber taunts of the youngest wife a
    craving in the roots of the eye-teeth
Makes a last effort a few steps

Snoring frowns of African bigshots, in the strobe glare
    and rumble of airports, uttering grunts of hard currency
Ballistic data in the inter-tribal Swahili of the Kalashnikov

The flies boom
Twenty-five pounds sterling feeds a family for ten weeks

The Black Rhino stands stock still is giddy

The thorny scrub has nothing to say. The waterholes are
silent. The horizon mountain-folds are silent.

The Black Rhino
Is vanishing

Into a soft
Human laugh

# Leaf Mould

In Hardcastle Crags, that echoey museum,
Where she dug leaf mould for her handfuls of garden
And taught you to walk, others are making poems.

*Between finger and thumb roll a pine-needle,*
*Feel the chamfer, feel how they threaded*
*The sewing machines.*
     And
*Billy Holt invented a new shuttle*
*As like an ant's egg, with its folded worker,*
*As every other.*
*You might see an ant carrying one.*
      And
*The cordite conscripts tramped away. But the cenotaphs*
*Of all the shells that got their heads blown off*
*And their insides blown out*
*Are these beech-bole stalwarts.*
      And oak, birch,
Holly, sycamore, pine.
        The lightest air-stir
Released their love-whispers when she walked
The needles weeping, singing, dedicating
Your spectre-double, still in her womb,
To this temple of her *Missa Solemnis*.

White-faced, brain-washed by her nostalgias,
You were her step-up transformer.
She grieved for her girlhood and the fallen.
You mourned for Paradise and its fable.

Giving you the kiss of life
She hung round your neck her whole valley
Like David's harp.
Now, whenever you touch it, God listens
Only for her voice.

Leaf mould. Blood-warm. Fibres crumbled alive
Between thumb and finger.
*Feel again*
*The clogs twanging your footsoles, on the street's steepness,*
*As you escaped.*

# Manchester Skytrain

Remember that nightmare straight into the camera—
Dice among dice, jounced in a jouncing cup.
Never any nearer, bouncing in a huddle, on the spot.
Struggling all together glued in a clot.

The first dead cert I ever backed was Word
From The Owner's Mouth. Week before
There was my jockey—'a day in the life of'—
Starred in *Picture Post*. Who? Somewhere

In the nineteen forty-seven
Strata of the British Museum.
He's gone. He went
Even as I watched. And the horse's name?

Gone with my money. It cartwheeled
Smack in front of me, over the first fence.
Left its jockey flat—killed—and galloped on
Long after the finish, in a drugged trance—

(Doncaster). One can't bear to be groomed:
Arcs into shudders, chewing at a scream.
One rolls on the ground and whirls hammers
Refusing to cross a stream,

Ending up shot. The stables—asylums
Of these blue-blooded insane—
Prefer the introverts. Here's one. A razor-faced
Big-eyed schizophrene.

Every known musical instrument,
The whole ensemble, packed
Into a top-heavy, twangling half ton
On the stilts of an insect.

They're all dangerous to touch. It nearly takes off—
Just stays. Like a flying saucer's
Anti-gravity coil magnet, still space-radioactive,
Eased hot from the wreck. It scares

Even itself. We stand, nervous. Metaphors
Fail the field of force.
Jokey disparagements
The torque of vertigo. A dark horse.

# Walt

*I. Under High Wood*

Going up for the assault that morning
They passed the enclosure of prisoners.
'A big German stood at the wire,' he said,
'A big German, and he caught my eye.
And he cursed me. I felt his eye curse me.'

Halfway up the field, the bullet
Hit him in the groin. He rolled
Into a shell-hole. The sun rose and burned.
A sniper clipped his forehead. He wormed
Deeper down. Bullet after bullet
Dug at the crater rim, searching for him.
Another clipped him. Then the sniper stopped.

All that day he lay. He went walks
Along the Heights Road, from Peckett to Midgley,
Down to Mytholmroyd (past Ewood
Of his ancestors, past the high-perched factory
Of his future life). Up the canal bank,
Up Redacre, along and down into Hebden,
Then up into Crimsworth Dene, to their old campground
In the happy valley,
And up over Shackleton Hill, to Widdop,
Back past Greenwood Lea, above Hardcastles,
To Heptonstall—all day
He walked about that valley, as he lay
Under High Wood in the shell-hole.

I knew the knot of scar on his temple.

We stood in the young March corn
Of a perfect field. His fortune made.
His life's hope over. Me beside him
Just the age he'd been when that German
Took aim with his eye and hit him so hard
It brought him and his wife down together,
With all his children one after the other.

A misty rain prickled and hazed.
'Here,' he hazarded. 'Somewhere just about here.
This is where he stopped me. I got this far.'

He frowned uphill towards the skyline tree-fringe
As through binoculars
Towards all that was left.

## II. *The Atlantic*

Night after night he'd sat there,
Eighty-four, still telling the tale.
With his huge thirst for anaesthetics.
'Time I were dead,' I'd heard. 'I want to die.'

That's altered.
                      We lean to a cliff rail
Founded in tremblings.
Beneath us, two thousand five hundred
Miles of swung worldweight
Hit England's western wall
With a meaningless bump.

'Aye!' he sighs. Over and over. 'Aye!'
And massages his temples.

Can he grasp what's happened? His frown
Won't connect. Familiar eagle frown—
Dark imperial eye. The ground flinches.
Mountains of dissolution
Boil cold geysers, bespatter us.
                                Tranquillizers,
Steroids, and a whole crateful
Of escapist Madeira, collided
Three evenings ago—

They swamped and drowned
The synapses, the breath-born spinnaker shells
Of consonants and vowels.

                              I found him
Trying to get up out of a chair,
Fish-eyed, and choking, clawing at air,
Dumbness like a bone stuck in his throat.

He's survived with a word—one last word.
A last mouthful. I listen.
And I almost hear a new baby's
Eyeless howl of outrage—sobered to 'Aye!'
Sighed slow. Like blessed breath. He breathes it.

I dare hardly look at him. I watch.
He'd crept into my care.
A cursed hulk of marriage, a full-rigged fortune
Cast his body, crusted like Job's,
Onto my threshold. Strange Dead Sea creature.
He crawled in his ruins, like Timon.
*The Times* Index was his morning torture.
Fairy gold of a family of dead leaves.
'Why?' he cried. 'Why can't I just die?'
His memory was so sharp—a potsherd.
He raked at his skin, whispering 'God! God!'
Nightly, a nurse eased his scales with ointment.

I've brought him out for air. And the cliffs. And there
The sea towards America—wide open.
Untrodden, glorious America!
Look, a Peregrine Falcon—they're rare!

Nothing will connect.
He peers down past his shoes
Into a tangle of horizons—

Black, tilted bedrock struggling up,
Mouthing disintegration.

Every weedy breath of the sea
Is another swell of overwhelming.
Meaningless. And a sigh. Meaningless.

Now he's closed his eyes. He caresses
His own skull, over and over, comforting.
The Millmaster, the Caesar whose frown
Tossed my boyhood the baffling coin 'guilty'.
His fingers are my mother's. They seem astray
In quaverings and loss
As he strokes and strokes at his dome.
The sea thuds and sighs. Bowed at the rail
He seems to be touching at a wound he dare not touch.
He seems almost to find the exact spot.
His eyelids quiver, in the certainty of touch—

And 'Aye!' he breathes. 'Aye!'

We turn away. Then as he steadies himself,
Still gripping the rail, his reaching stare
Meets mine watching him. I can't escape it

Or hold it. Walt! Walt!

                               I bury it

Hugger-mugger anyhow
Inside my shirt.

# Take What You Want But Pay For It

*I.*

Weary of the cries
God spoke to the Soul of Adam
Saying: 'Give me your body.' And He
Took Adam's body and nailed it
To a stake, saying: 'This great beast
Shall destroy your peace no more.'

Then God fortified with buttresses
His house's walls, and so devised a prison
For the contorted body
Of the beast. Outside, the Soul, in a shroud,
Glorified the Majesty
Of the defensive structure, towards which
It fled from the enclosing
And unappeasable cry
Of the surrounding bush. Once inside
The locked sanctuary and seeing
Its own body nailed down
To silence, harmless, and
No longer thirsting, it wept
Astounded at the finished and cold
Beauty of its own torment
And the stony peace
Cupped it like hands, and breathed into it
Grace. No longer life,
Simply Grace, whispering: 'This is Grace.'

*II.*

Then the Soul of Adam
Gasped as if in airlessness and there came
In from his hands and feet up through
His bowels and in
Through his shoulders and down
From all the sutures of his skull a single
Cry braiding together all the uncried

Cries his body could no longer cry
A single flagellant thong
With which he drove his ghostly being shuddering
Back into the body and
In that sudden inrush of renewal
The nailed feet and the hands
Tore free of the nails and he fell
From the emptied gibbet to earth

And tried to rise and raised
His blood-anointed head and tried to cry
But could not move. Only raised
The blood-mask and its effort
In his broken attempt to get up.
Then God withdrew, horrified
Almost afraid, as He saw

Exhaling from the black pits
Of each nail hole and from each gouged
Inscription of blood an ectoplasm
Bluish, and from the blackest pit of all

That issued the despair and its noise
A misty enfoldment which materialized
As a musing woman, who lifted the body
As a child's, effortless, and walked
Out of the prison with it, singing gently

## Us He Devours

The long Shrine of hunger. Window spectra
Bleak on the retina. It is the hunger
Humbles the eye-beam.

The slime's Great Orme. Stranded, immense Mollusk!
A carapace of stone, cruciform,
Sculpted, as are all God's creatures, by hunger.

Gill-arches high and dry—
It filters
The breath off the water's face, the salt airs.

Casualty of a peculiar cry:
Eloi Eloi
Which is the only sound it ever utters.

That near-fatal cry alone sustains it.

Calling to the eye of the mind
A lost orphan Lamb
For whom the mouth is a wound.

The spiral nebulae that have turned
Into howlings and gnashings.
And the tiny bird of January

Who flees tap-tapping at every bud in the orchard
With such anguish, such foregone despair
It finds nothing, or barely enough

To keep it alive to its pang and that echoing
Immanence of famine.
The four-inch triangle

Of imperishable artefact that furnished
The gape of *Megalodon*
*Carcharadon* in the first seas.

The insupportable sun. A gargoyle
(Empty gullet, condemned in stone,
Gulping at the elixirs of damnation)

To which lichens of Gothic adhere lightly.

# Little Whale Song

*for Charles Causley*

What do they think of themselves
With their global brains—
The tide-power voltage illumination
Of those brains? Their X-ray all-dimension

Grasp of this world's structures, their brains budded
Clone replicas of the electron world
Lit and re-imagining the world,
Perfectly tuned receivers and perceivers,

Each one a whole tremulous world
Feeling through the world? What
Do they make of each other?

'We are beautiful. We stir

Our self-colour in the pot of colours
Which is the world. At each
Tail-stroke we deepen
Our being into the world's lit substance,

And our joy into the world's
Spinning bliss, and our peace
Into the world's floating, plumed peace.'

Their body-tons, echo-chambered,

Amplify the whisper
Of currents and airs, of sea-peoples

And planetary manoeuvres,
Of seasons, of shores, and of their own

Moon-lifted incantation, as they dance
Through the original Earth-drama
In which they perform, as from the beginning,
The Royal House.
                          The loftiest, spermiest

Passions, the most exquisite pleasures,
The noblest characters, the most god-like
Oceanic presence and poise—

The most terrible fall.

# On the Reservations

*for Jack Brown*

*I. Sitting Bull on Christmas Morning*

Who put this pit-head wheel,
Smashed but carefully folded
In some sooty fields, into his stocking?
And this lifetime nightshift—a snarl
Of sprung celluloid? Here's his tin flattened,
His helmet. And the actual sun closed
Into what looks like a bible of coal
That falls to bits as he lifts it. Very strange.
Packed in mossy woods, mostly ashes,
Here's a doll's cot. And a tiny coffin.

And here are Orca Tiger Eagle tattered
In his second birthday's ragbook
From before memory began.
All the props crushed, the ceilings collapsed
In his stocking. Torremolinos, Cleethorpes—
The brochures screwed up in a tantrum
As her hair shrivelled to a cinder
In his stocking. Pit boots. And, strange,
A London, burst, spewing tea-leaves,
With a creased postcard of the Acropolis.

Chapels pews broken television.
(Who dumped these, into his stocking,
Under coal-slag in a flooded cellar?)
*Pink Uns* and a million whippet collars—
Did he ask for these? A jumbo jet

Parcelled in starred, split, patched Christmas wrappings
Of a concrete yard and a brick wall
Black with scribble
In his stocking. No tobacco. A few
Rabbits and foxes broken leaking feathers.

Nevertheless, he feels like a new man—

Though tribally scarred (stitch-tattoos of coal-dust),
Though pale (soiled, the ivory bulb of a snowdrop
Dug up and tossed aside),
Though one of the lads (the horde, the spores of nowhere
Cultured under lamps and multiplied
In the laboratories
Between Mersey and Humber),
He stands, lungs easy, freed hands—

Bombarded by pollens from the supernovae,
Two eyepits awash in the millennia—

With his foot in his stocking.

## II. Nightvoice

*My young men shall never work. Men who work cannot
dream, and wisdom comes in dreams.*
—Smohalla, Nez Percé Indians

She dreams she sleepwalks crying the Don River
relieves its nine
circles through her kitchen her kids
mops and brooms herself a squeegee and not
soaking in but
bulging pulsing out of their pores the
ordure *déjà vu* in Tesco's makes her
giddy

She dreams she sleepwalks crying her Dad alive
dug up is being
pushed into a wood-burning stove
by pensioners who chorus in croaks
While Shepherds
Watched Their television gives her
palpitations

She dreams she sleepwalks crying all the dead
huddle
in the slag-heaps wrong
land wrong
time tepees a final
resting for the epidemic
solution every
pit-shaft a

mass-grave herself
in a silly bottle shawled
in the canal's
fluorescence the message
of the survivors   a surplus people
the words
washed off her wrists
and hands she complains keep feeling
helpless

She dreams she sleepwalks mainstreet nightly crying
Stalin
keeps her as an ant
in a formicary in a
garbage-can which is his private office
urinal she thinks her aerials
must be bent

Remembering how a flare of pure torrent
sluiced the pit muck
off his shoulder-slopes while her hands
soapy with milk blossom anointed
him and in their hearth
fingers of the original sun opened
the black
bright book of the stone
he'd brought from beneath dreams
or did she dream it

## III. The Ghost Dancer

*We are not singing sportive songs. It is as if*
*we were weeping, asking for life—*
*—Owl, Fox Indians*

A sulky boy. And he stuns your ear with song.
Swastika limbs, his whole physique—a dance.
The fool of prophecy, nightlong, daylong
Out of a waste lot brings deliverance.

Just some kid, with a demonic roar
Spinning *in vacuo*, inches clear of the floor.

Half-anguish half-joy, half-shriek half-moan:
He is the gorgon against his own fear.
Through his septum a dog's penile bone.
A chime of Chubb keys dangling at each ear.

Temenos Jaguar mask—a vogue mandala:
Half a Loa, half a drugged Oglala.

With woad cobras coiling their arm-clasp
Out of his each arm-pit, their ganch his grasp.

Bracelets, anklets; girlish, a bacchus chained.
An escapologist's pavement, padlock dance.
A mannequin elf, topped with a sugarfloss mane
Or neon rhino power-cone on a shorn sconce,

Or crest of a Cock of the Rock, or Cockatoo shock,
Or the sequinned crown of a Peacock.

And snake-spined, all pentecostal shivers,
This megawatt, berserker medium
With his strobe-drenched battle-cry delivers
The nineteenth century from his mother's womb:

The work-house dread that brooded, through her term,
Over the despair of salvaged sperm.

Mau-Mau Messiah's showbiz lightning stroke
Puffs the stump of Empire up in smoke.

Brain-box back to front, heart inside out,
Aura for body, and for so-called soul
Under the moment's touch a reed that utters
Out of the solar cobalt core a howl

Bomb-lit, rainbowed, aboriginal:
'Start afresh, this time unconquerable.'

## A Dove

Snaps its twig-tether—mounts—
Dream-yanked up into vacuum
Wings snickering.

Another, in a shatter, hurls dodging away up.

They career through tree-mazes—
Nearly uncontrollable love-weights.

Or now
Temple-dancers, possessed, and steered
By solemn powers
Through insane, stately convulsions.

Porpoises
Of dove-lust and blood splendour
With arcs
And plungings, and spray-slow explosions.

Now violently gone
Riding the snake of the long love-whip
Among flarings of mares and stallions

Now staying
Coiled on a bough
Bubbling molten, wobbling top-heavy
Into one and many.

# Notes

'The Black Rhino' (*page 30*): This piece was written to help raise funds for the campaign to save the Black Rhinoceros.

By 1980 the formerly vast numbers of African Black Rhino had been reduced to about seventeen thousand. From earliest times, India and all countries eastward of it have regarded the rhino, and especially its horn, as a cornucopia of magical, versatile medicines. Modern marketing has increased the value of the horn at the point of sale, in the East, to three times its weight in gold, and modern weapons have supplied the trade. As much horn again goes to North Yemen, where the outcome of the Civil War combined with the oil crisis to produce a freakish, mass market for the costly rhino-horn-handled *djambia*, the ceremonial curved Yemenite dagger.

In 1986, when the Black Rhino population in Africa was diving towards four thousand, the English writer Martin Booth visited the South Luangwa National Park in Zambia to reconnoitre for a film about the Black Rhino's plight. This park was known at the time to hold one of the densest concentrations of surviving Black Rhino, and the particular region he surveyed held 'upwards of thirty', nearly all identified. Among these he located one large old bull, whom he hoped to make the star of his film. In September 1987, when he went back there with his film crew (and while I was composing this piece), he couldn't find a single Black Rhino. The 'upwards of thirty' of the year before had been reduced to an untraceable 'perhaps three'. He recapitulated the opening section of my poem by finding the skeleton of his old rhino bull.

'On the Reservations' (*page 56*): The general setting here is the industrial region of the North of England, across South Yorkshire and South Lancashire. In particular, my piece relates to the South

Yorkshire coalfields (devastated one way by the growth of the industry, now another way by its collapse) drained by the watershed of the river Don, where I passed most of my schooldays.